Zaner-Bloser
Handwriting
With a simplified alphabet

Author

Clinton S. Hackney

Contributing Authors

Pamela J. Farris
Janice T. Jones
Linda Leonard Lamme

Zaner-Bloser, Inc.
P.O. Box 16764
Columbus, Ohio 43216-6764

Author

Clinton S. Hackney, Ed.D.

Contributing Authors

Pamela J. Farris, Ph.D.
Janice T. Jones, M.A.
Linda Leonard Lamme, Ph.D.

Reviewers

Judy L. Bausch, Columbus, Georgia

Cherlynn Bruce, Conroe, Texas

Karen H. Burke, Director of Curriculum and Instruction, Bar Mills, Maine

Anne Chamberlin, Lynchburg, Virginia

Carol J. Fuhler, Flagstaff, Arizona

Deborah D. Gallagher, Gainesville, Florida

Kathleen Harrington, Redford, Michigan

Rebecca James, East Greenbush, New York

Gerald R. Maeckelbergh, Principal, Blaine, Minnesota

Bessie B. Peabody, Principal, East St. Louis, Illinois

Marilyn S. Petruska, Coraopolis, Pennsylvania

Sharon Ralph, Nashville, Tennessee

Linda E. Ritchie, Birmingham, Alabama

Roberta Hogan Royer, North Canton, Ohio

Marion Redmond Starks, Baltimore, Maryland

Elizabeth J. Taglieri, Lake Zurich, Illinois

Claudia Williams, Lewisburg, West Virginia

Credits

Art: Liz Callen: 3, 26–27, 29, 42–43, 45, 64–65, 71, 86–87, 101, 106; Gloria Elliott: 5, 16, 58, 96; Michael Grejniec: 1, 3, 6–7, 20–21, 34–35, 37, 44, 50–53, 56–57, 72–73, 82–83, 94, 99, 110; Rosekrans Hoffman: 3, 30–31, 46–47, 58, 62–63, 76–77, 85, 90, 100, 105; Andy San Diego: 3, 5, 16–19, 32–33, 48–49, 59–61, 70, 80–81, 84, 92–93, 102; Troy Viss: 3, 12–13, 24–25, 28, 36, 40–41, 66–67, 78–79, 88–89, 96, 104, 108–109; John Wallner: 22–23, 38–39, 68–69, 74–75, 91, 103, 107

Photos: John Lei/OPC: 8–9, 97; Stephen Ogilvy: 3–4, 7, 10–11, 13–15, 20–21, 24–25, 29, 32–33, 36, 38–39, 42, 46–47, 50, 55, 56–57, 60–63, 65–68, 71–73, 75–77, 79–83, 86–89, 91–93, 95, 97–99, 101, 105, 107–109, 110

Developed by Kirchoff/Wohlberg, Inc., in cooperation with Zaner-Bloser Publishers

Cover illustration by Michael Grejniec

ISBN 0-88085-948-2

07 08 09 (159) 20 19 18 17 16

CONTENTS

Unit I Getting Started

Unit 2 Writing Lowercase Letters

Unit 3 Writing Uppercase Letters

Unit 4 Using Cursive Writing

cool

If you can read this word, you're ready to write in cursive.

In cursive writing, letters are joined to other letters. In this book, you will learn how to write cursive letters, how to join the letters to write words, and how to space the words to write sentences. You will learn how to make your writing easy to read.

So Much
I have so much to say
And so much to write.
I want every word
To be written just right!

So Much
I have so much to say
And so much to write.
I want every word
To be written just right!

So Much

I have so much to say
And so much to write.
I want every word
To be written just right!

So Much
I have so much to say
And so much to write.
I want every word
To be written just right!

So Much
I have so much to say
And so much to write.
I want every word
To be written just right!

So Much
I have so much to say
And so much to write.
I want every word
To be written just right!

Write the poem in your best handwriting.

Circle your best line of writing.

Left-Handed Writers

If you are left-handed . . .

Sit up tall. Place both arms on the table. Keep your feet flat on the floor. This way, your body will be well balanced.

Hold your pencil with your first two fingers and your thumb. Point the pencil toward your left elbow.

Your paper should slant with the lower right corner pointing toward you. Pull your downstrokes toward your left elbow. Then you can make your writing slant the way you want it to.

Right-Handed Writers

If you are right-handed . . .

Sit up tall. Place both arms on the table. Keep your feet flat on the floor. This way, your body will be well balanced.

Hold your pencil with your first two fingers and your thumb. Point the pencil toward your right shoulder.

Your paper should slant with the lower left corner pointing toward you. Pull your downstrokes toward your midsection. Then you can make your writing slant the way you want it to.

Lowercase Cursive Letters and Numerals

aa bb cc dd ee ff gg

hh ii jj kk ll mm nn

oo pp qq rr ss tt uu

vv ww xx yy zz

1 2 3 4 5 6 7 8 9 10

Circle the lowercase cursive letters that are in your name.

How are these manuscript and cursive words different?

handwriting

handwriting

Uppercase Cursive Letters

A A   B B   C C   D D   E E   F F   G G
H H   I I   J J   K K   L L   M M   N N
O O   P P   Q Q   R R   S S   T T   U U
V V   W W   X X   Y Y   Z Z   ! !   ? ?

Circle your cursive initials.

Circle the cursive letter that begins the name of your state.

How are these sentences different?

Ben moved to Tampa.

Ben moved to Tampa.

Reading Cursive Writing

Read the card. Write the words in manuscript under
each cursive phrase.

Happy birthday,

Happy birthday,

Happy birthday to you.

How old are you?

_____

_____

How old are you?

_____

_____

How old are you now?

_____

_____

I am 8.

I am 9.

How old is she?

Important Strokes for Cursive Writing

Undercurves swing,
Downcurves dive,
Overcurves bounce,
Slants just slide.

Undercurve

Write undercurve strokes.

Downcurve

Write downcurve strokes.

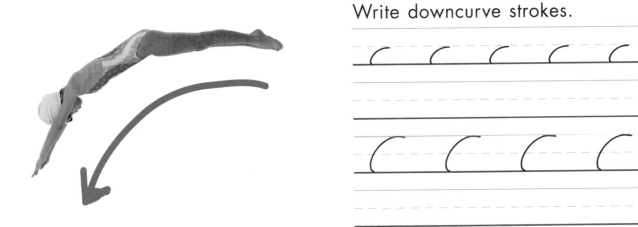

Undercurve, downcurve,
Overcurve, slant.
As you write cursive letters,
Remember this chant.

Overcurve

Write overcurve strokes.

Slant

Write slant strokes.

Before You Go On . . .

You've got to start somewhere!

Writing Lowercase Letters

Begin here. Circle the lowercase letters that are written in cursive.

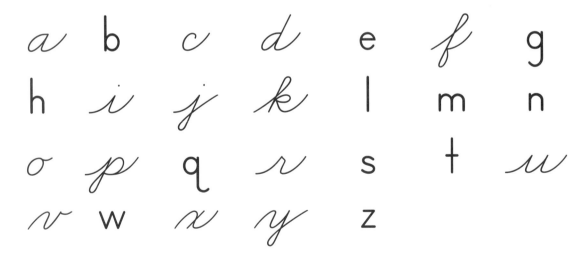

a b c d e f g
h i j k l m n
o p q r s t u
v w x y z

In the following pages, you will write all the lowercase letters in cursive. You will pay attention to the size and shape of letters to help make your writing easy to read.

Keys to Legibility: Size and Shape

Help make your writing easy to read.
Pay attention to the size and shape of lowercase letters.

Tall letters touch the headline.

Short letters touch the midline.

Letters with descenders go below the baseline.

Look at the letters below. Circle the green letters that are the correct size and shape.

Circle i and *i* in these words.

pigs in wigs eating spaghetti

pigs in wigs eating spaghetti

Trace and write.

i   i

Write *i*.

i   i   i   i   i

Join *i* and *i*.

ii   ii   ii   ii

Circle your best *i*.

a tower of tigers in tutus

a tower of tigers in tutus

Circle t and *t* in these words.

Trace and write.

t   t

Write *t*.

t   t   t   t   t

Join *t* and other letters.

tt   tt   tt   tt

ti   ti   ti   ti

Circle your best *t*.

Write the word *it*.

it   it   it   it

19

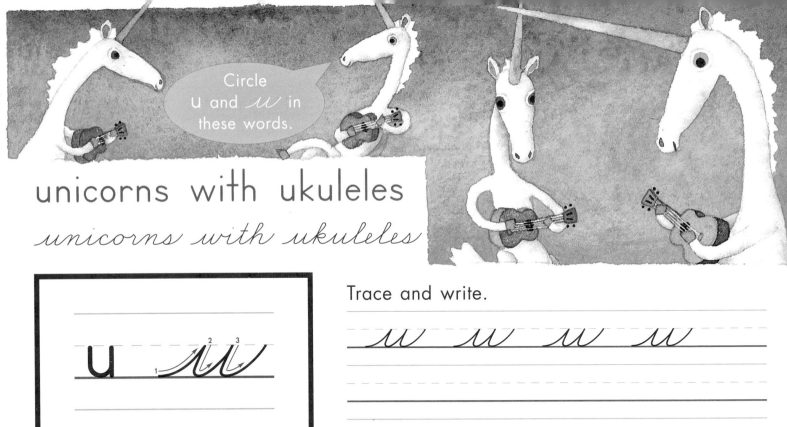

Circle u and *u* in these words.

unicorns with ukuleles

unicorns with ukuleles

u *uu*

Trace and write.

uu   uu   uu   uu

Write *u*.

uu   uu   uu   uu   uu   uu

Join *u* and other letters.

ut   ut   tu   tu   uit

Write words with *u*.

tut   tutu

Circle your best *u*.

Circle W and *w* in these words.

walruses washing watermelons

walruses washing watermelons

W *w*

Trace and write.

w   w   w   w

Write *w*.

w   w   w   w   w   w

Join *w* and other letters.

wi   wu   wt   tw   iw

Write the word *wit*.

wit   wit

Circle your best *w*.

21

Review

Write these letter joinings.

ti   tu   tw   twi

ui   ut   uit

wi   wt   wu

Circle your best joining.

Write these words.

it   wit   tut   tutu

Circle your best word.

22

rhinos riding rubber rafts
rhinos riding rubber rafts

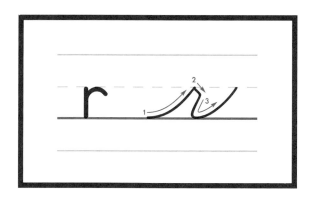

Trace and write.

r r

Write *r*.

r r r r r

Join *r* and other letters.

ri ru rt wr

wri ir urt

Write words with *r*.

rut writ

Circle r and *r* in these words.

Circle your best *r*.

storks in striped sweaters

storks in striped sweaters

Circle S and *s* in these words.

S

Trace and write.

s s s s s

Write *s*.

s s s s s s s

Join *s* and other letters.

si su st sw rs

Circle your best *s*.

Write words with *s*.

stir suit its

24

porcupines playing the piano

porcupines playing the piano

Trace and write.

p   p   p   p   p

Write *p*.

p   p   p   p   p   p

Join *p* **and other letters.**

pi   pu   pr   ps   rp   sp

Write words with *p*.

pit   purr   pups

Circle j and *j* in these words.

jumping jaguars in pajamas

jumping jaguars in pajamas

j *j*

Trace and write.

j j

Write *j*.

j   j   j   j   j

Join *j* and other letters.

ji   jit   ju   uj

jui   jus   jur

Circle your best *j*.

Write words with *j*.

jut   just   juts

Review

r s p j

Circle your best joining.

Write these letter joinings.

rs rp sp pr ju

Write these words.

sip tip trip suit

just rust spur

Circle your best word.

wrist twists

27

Manuscript Maintenance: Compound Words

Join each word in the first column with a word in the second column to form a new word.

ant	shoe
dragon	fish
grass	house
cow	eater
jelly	neck
horse	hopper
turtle	fly
dog	hand

Write the new words in your best manuscript.

Circle *a* and *a* in these words.

anteaters in armor

anteaters in armor

a *a*

Trace and write.

a   a   a   a

Write *a*.

a   a   a   a   a   a   a

Join *a* and other letters.

ai   ap   arp   ast   wa

Circle your best *a*.

Write words with *a*.

air   jar   upstairs

29

Circle C and c in these words.

cats on a cable car

cats on a cable car

C c

Trace and write.

c   c

Write c.

c   c   c   c   c   c

Join c and other letters.

ca ci cu scr ct

Write words with c.

circus   cactus

cats   scrap   act

Circle your best c.

dancing dogs in derbies

dancing dogs in derbies

d d

Circle d and *d* in these words.

Trace and write.

d *d*

Write *d*.

d d d d d d

Join *d* and other letters.

di da du dr id

Write words with *d*.

draw did dust

card aid add

Circle your best *d*.

Circle q and *q* in these words.

a quintet of quick quails

a quintet of quick quails

Trace and write.

q   q   q   q   q

Write *q*.

q   q   q   q   q   q   q

Join *q* and other letters.

qu   squ   qua   qui

Circle your best *q*.

Write words with *q*.

quart   quits   squirt

Circle g and *g* in these words.

a gaggle of geese in goggles

a gaggle of geese in goggles

g *g*

Trace and write.

g   g   g   g   g

Write *g*.

g   g   g   g   g   g   g

Join *g* and other letters.

ga   gi   gu   gr   ag

Write words with *g*.

grip   guitar   dug

Circle your best *g*.

ostriches in an opera

ostriches in an opera

Circle **O** and $\mathcal{O}$ in these words.

Circle your best $\mathcal{O}$.

Trace and write.

$\mathcal{O}$ $\mathcal{O}$ $\mathcal{O}$

Write $\mathcal{O}$.

$\mathcal{O}$ $\mathcal{O}$ $\mathcal{O}$ $\mathcal{O}$ $\mathcal{O}$ $\mathcal{O}$

Join $\mathcal{O}$ and other letters.

oo oi oa ou ot

Write words with $\mathcal{O}$.

post soap stood

across curious

34

Review

Write these words.

carrot   potato   toast

cat   quit   dog   cow

Write these phrases.

two proud actors

Circle your best word.

coast to coast

35

Numerals

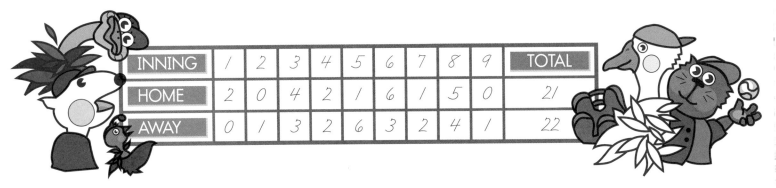

INNING	1	2	3	4	5	6	7	8	9	TOTAL
HOME	2	0	4	2	1	6	1	5	0	21
AWAY	0	1	3	2	6	3	2	4	1	22

Write numerals.

1   2   3   4   5   6   7   8   9   10

Look at the scoreboard. Then fill in the missing numerals on the scorecard.

INNING	1	2		4		6	7		9	TOTAL
HOME	2	0		2	1	6	1	5	0	
AWAY	0	1	3	2		3		4		22

How many runs were scored in the fifth inning?

How many runs were scored in the eighth inning?

How many runs were scored in the first three innings combined?

Circle your best numeral.

36

a band of noisy nightingales

a band of noisy nightingales

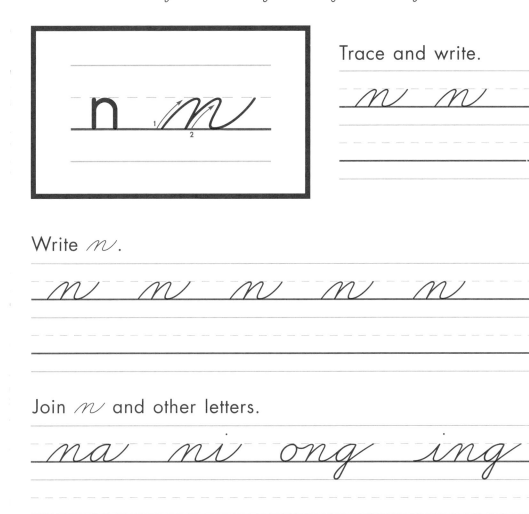

n m

Trace and write.

n   m

Write n.

n   n   n   n   n

Join n and other letters.

na   ni   ong   ing

Write words with n.

narrow   again

song   stopping

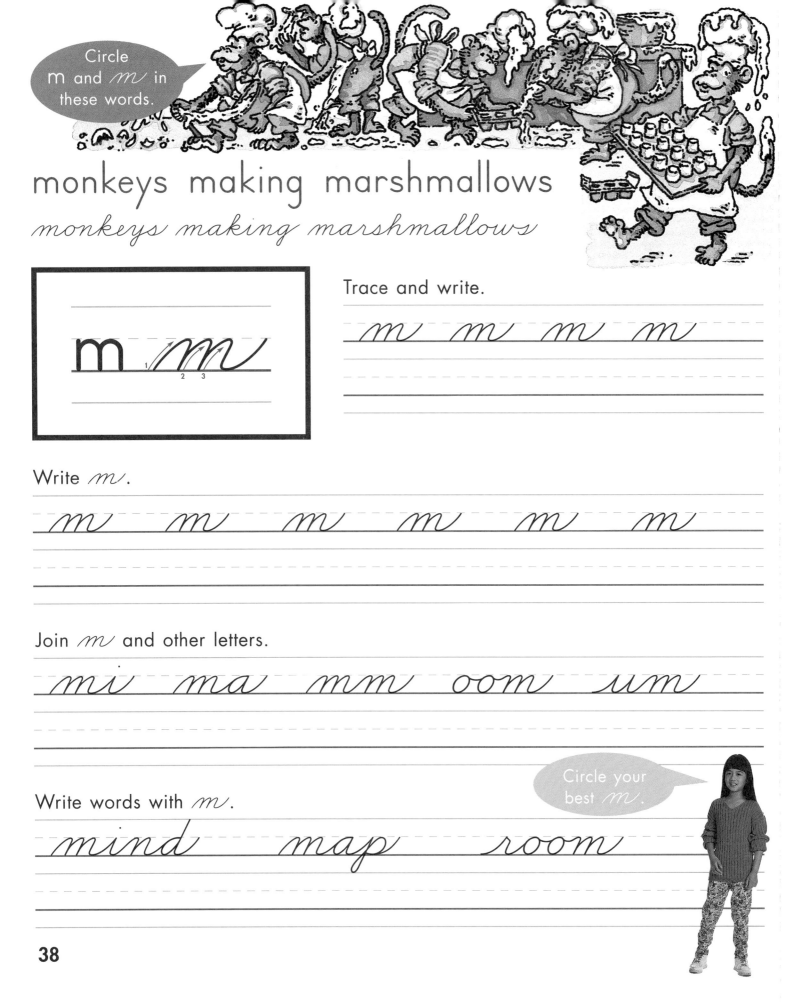

Circle m and *m* in these words.

monkeys making marshmallows

monkeys making marshmallows

m *m*

Trace and write.

m   m   m   m

Write *m*.

m   m   m   m   m   m

Join *m* and other letters.

mi   ma   mm   oom   um

Circle your best *m*.

Write words with *m*.

mind   map   room

Circle X and x in these words.

foxes fixing a taxi

foxes fixing a taxi

X x

Trace and write.

x x x x

Write x.

x x x x x x x

Join x and other letters.

xa xi ax ix ixt

Write words with x.

mixing taxi ox

Circle your best x.

39

yaks playing with yo-yos

Circle y and *y* in these words.

Circle your best *y*.

Trace and write.

y y

Write *y*.

y   y   y   y   y

Join *y* and other letters.

ya   yo   ys   ay   oy

Write words with *y*.

yard   carry

yours   says

zebras zipping zippers

zebras zipping zippers

Trace and write.

Write *z*.

Join *z* and other letters.

zi zo zy az iz

Write words with *z*.

dizzy quiz jazz

zooms zigzag

Circle Z and *z* in these words.

Circle your best *z*.

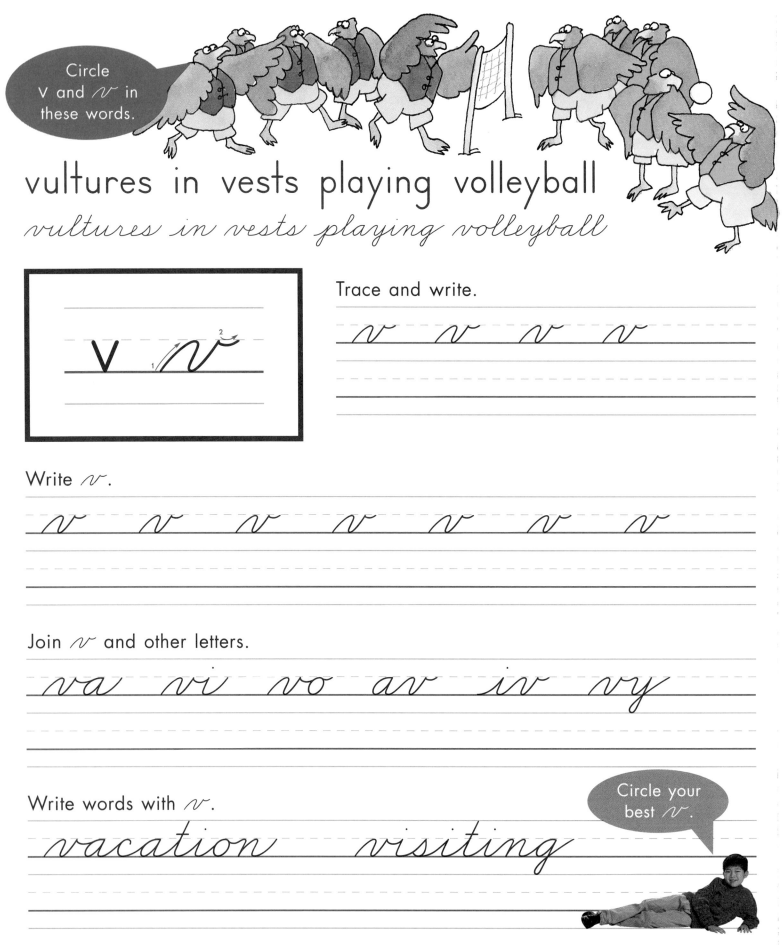

Circle V and *v* in these words.

vultures in vests playing volleyball

vultures in vests playing volleyball

Trace and write.

Write *v*.

Join *v* and other letters.

va   vi   vo   av   iv   vy

Write words with *v*.

vacation   visiting

Circle your best *v*.

42

Review

n m x y z v

Write these words.

morning   *noon*   *gravy*

zooming   *mix*

Write these phrases.

sixty moving vans

six amazing toys

Circle your best word.

Manuscript Maintenance: Word Search

Find the animal names in the Word Search. The words may go across or down. Then write them using your best uppercase manuscript.

STORK

JAGUAR

CAT

FOX

TIGER

YAK

A	C	S	J	F	D
C	A	P	A	X	J
R	T	I	G	E	R
D	O	G	U	Y	O
F	O	X	A	A	Z
S	T	O	R	K	Q

PIG

DOG

ACROSS

DOWN

electric eels on an escalator

electric eels on an escalator

e ℓ

Trace and write.

ℓ ℓ

Write ℓ.

ℓ ℓ ℓ ℓ ℓ

Join ℓ and other letters.

ea ee en ew ie

Write words with ℓ.

enjoy east

new everyone

Circle e and ℓ in these words.

Circle your best ℓ.

45

Circle l and *l* in these words.

llamas logrolling on a lake

llamas logrolling on a lake

Trace and write.

l   l   l   l   l   l   l

Write *l*.

l   l   l   l   l   l   l   l

Join *l* **and other letters.**

la   le   lo   al   ly   ll

Circle your best *l*.

Write words with *l*.

lovely   always   list

Circle h and *h* in these words.

hyenas honking their horns
hyenas honking their horns

Trace and write.

h   h   h   h

Write *h*.

h   h   h   h   h   h

Join *h* and other letters.

hea   ho   hu   chy   sh   th

Write words with *h*.

healthy   hotter

Circle your best *h*.

47

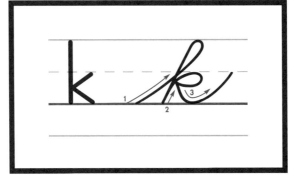

kangaroos in kilts flying kites

kangaroos in kilts flying kites

Circle k and *k* in these words.

Circle your best *k*.

k

Trace and write.

k k

Write *k*.

k   k   k   k

Join *k* and other letters.

ke kn ka ck

Write words with *k*.

kind knew desk

quick kept joke

a flamingo family pulling taffy

a flamingo family pulling taffy

f / f

Circle f and *f* in these words.

Trace and write.

f f

Write *f*.

f f f f f

Join *f* and other letters.

fa fi fo fl ffy

Write words with *f*.

family   forest

half   foxes

Circle your best *f*.

49

baboons blowing bubbles

baboons blowing bubbles

Trace and write.

Write *b*.

Join *b* and other letters.

ba   bea   by   bo   ub

Write words with *b*.

because   bought

Review

Write these words.

football   flock   fact

behind   above   below

Write these phrases.

breakfast and lunch

Circle your best word.

umbrellas for sale

In Other Words

English

cap

French

casquette

Spanish

gorro

Other Languages

English

ball

French

balle

Spanish

pelota

Other Languages

English

apple

French

pomme

Spanish

manzana

Other Languages

English

watermelon

French

pastèque

Spanish

sandía

Other Languages

Review Lowercase Letters

a   b   c   d   e   f   g

n   o   p   q   r   s   t

Write these lowercase letters in cursive.

t w p r

i j s u

c o a g d q

m n x v z y

b k h f e l

Write these words in cursive.

busy

true

junk

view

excited

porch

giraffe

maze

queen

hello

h   i   j   k   l   m

u   v   w   x   y   z

Change the order of the letters to write a new word.

tab   *foal*   *chin*

gum   *rate*   *peal*

Change the first letter to write a new word.

moat   *fill*   *cast*

Circle your best word.

get   *pay*   *bell*

Joinings

Write each joining.

li   et   cu   pe

eg   na   rm   dy

ze   gi   yo   ja

gn   zy   br   wi

Circle your best joining.

va   bo   ov   wn

56

Write these words.

often   jumping

yellow   brought

friends   another

cave   xylophone

unable   trick

Circle your best joining in each word.

Put an **x** under a joining that could be better.

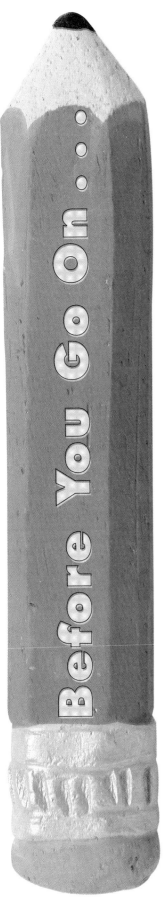

y name is abbit.

What's wrong with this picture?

Writing Uppercase Letters

You use uppercase letters to begin names and sentences. Circle the uppercase letters in your first and last names.

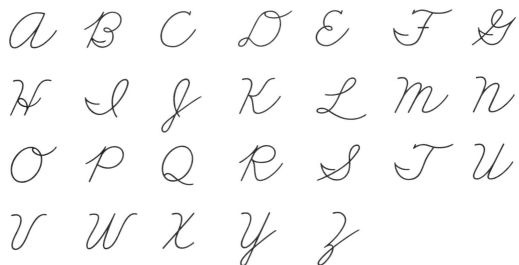

In the following pages, you will write uppercase cursive letters in names and sentences. You will pay attention to the size and shape of letters to help make your writing easy to read.

Keys to Legibility: Size and Shape

Help make your writing easy to read.
Pay attention to the size and shape of uppercase letters.

All uppercase letters are tall letters.

$\mathcal{J}$, $\mathcal{Y}$, and $\mathcal{Z}$ are letters with descenders.

Look at the letters below.
Circle the green letters
that are the correct size
and shape.

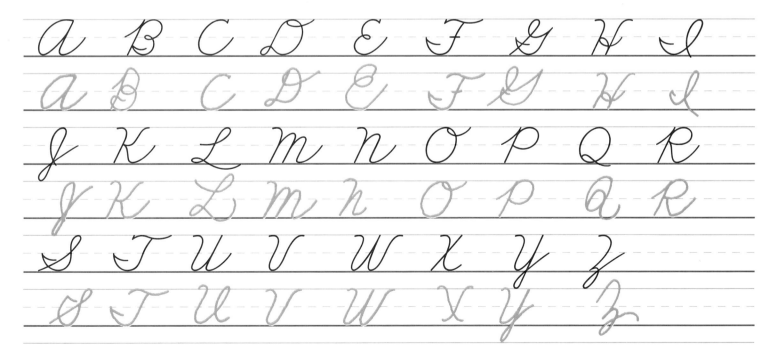

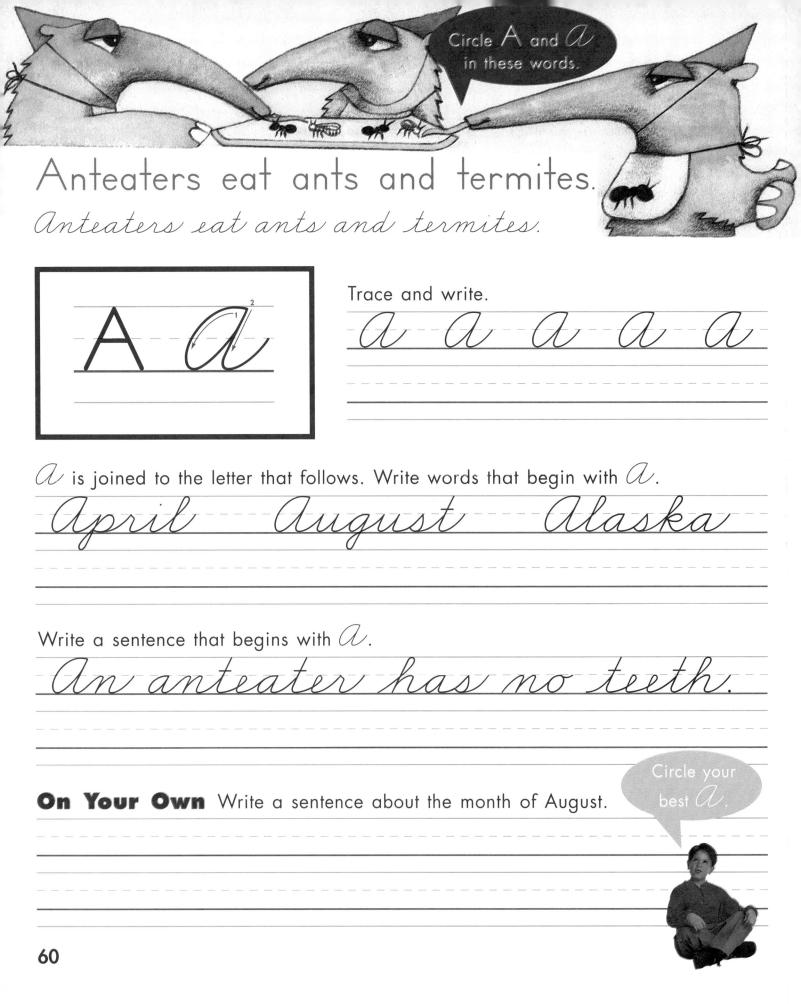

Circle A and *a* in these words.

Anteaters eat ants and termites.

Anteaters eat ants and termites.

A a

Trace and write.

a   a   a   a   a

a is joined to the letter that follows. Write words that begin with *a*.

April   August   Alaska

Write a sentence that begins with *a*.

An anteater has no teeth.

On Your Own Write a sentence about the month of August.

Circle your best *a*.

60

Coyotes howl at night.

Coyotes howl at night.

Trace and write.

C C C C C C

C is joined to the letter that follows. Write words that begin with *C*.

Canada   Celsius   Craig

Write a sentence that begins with *C*.

Certain coyotes eat fruit.

On Your Own Write a sentence about Canada.

Circle your best *C*.

Circle E and E in these words.

Elephants have ivory tusks.

Elephants have ivory tusks.

E E

Trace and write.

E E E E E E

E is joined to the letter that follows. Write words that begin with E.

Earth   Erie   English

Write a sentence that begins with E.

Elephants have trunks.

On Your Own Write a sentence about elephants.

Circle your best E.

62

Circle O and O in these words.

Ostriches are the largest birds.

Ostriches are the largest birds.

Trace and write.

O O O O O

O is not joined to the letter that follows. Write words that begin with O.

October Olympics Oki

Write a sentence that begins with O.

Ostriches live in Africa.

On Your Own Write a sentence that begins with O.

Circle your best O.

Review

Write names of mountain ranges.

Andes   Oeta   Catskill

Elburz   Ozark   Alps

Write these sentences.

Oya saw the Andes.

Circle your best word.

Ed likes the Cascades.

64

Nightingales migrate to Africa.

Nightingales migrate to Africa.

Circle N and n in these words.

N n

Trace and write.

n n n n n

n is joined to the letter that follows. Write words that begin with n.

November Neptune Nat

Write a sentence that begins with n.

Not all nightingales sing.

On Your Own Write a sentence about the planet Neptune.

Circle your best n.

65

Circle M and *m* in these words.

Monkeys sleep in trees.

Monkeys sleep in trees.

M m

Trace and write.

m m m m m

m is joined to the letter that follows. Write words that begin with *m*.

March May Monday

Write a sentence that begins with *m*.

Most monkeys have tails.

On Your Own Write a sentence about Monday.

Circle your best *m*.

66

Circle K and *K* in these words.

Kangaroos hop on their hind legs.

Kangaroos hop on their hind legs.

Trace and write.

K K K K K K K

K is joined to the letter that follows. Write words that begin with *K*.

Kansas   Kentucky   Kyle

Write a sentence that begins with *K*.

Kangaroos have big ears.

On Your Own Write a sentence about kangaroos.

Circle your best *K*.

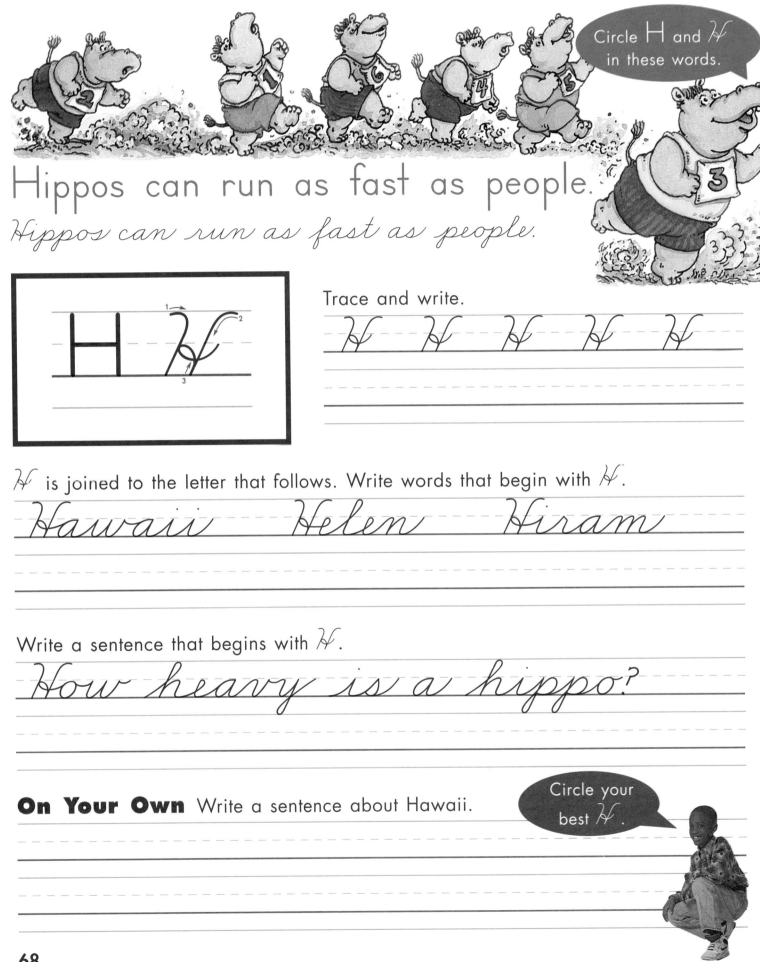

Circle H and *H* in these words.

Hippos can run as fast as people.

Hippos can run as fast as people.

Trace and write.

H H H H H

H is joined to the letter that follows. Write words that begin with *H*.

Hawaii   Helen   Hiram

Write a sentence that begins with *H*.

How heavy is a hippo?

On Your Own Write a sentence about Hawaii.

Circle your best *H*.

Review

Write names of rivers in the United States.

Missouri Kentucky Neosho

Mississippi   Hudson

Write these sentences.

How long is the Neosho?

Meet Ki at the river.

Circle your best word.

69

Manuscript Maintenance: Palindromes

A palindrome is a word, phrase, or sentence that is spelled exactly the same forward and backward.

Write these palindromes in your best manuscript.

wow   pup   eye   did   noon   peep

Bob   Otto   Hannah

Step on no pets.   Was it a cat I saw?

On Your Own Write a palindrome of your own.

Circle U and 𝒰 in these words.

Unicorns have only one horn.

Unicorns have only one horn.

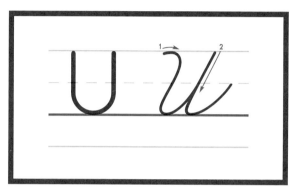

Trace and write.

𝒰   𝒰   𝒰   𝒰   𝒰

𝒰 is joined to the letter that follows. Write words that begin with 𝒰.

Utah   Uranus   Uma

Write a sentence that begins with 𝒰.

Unicorns are not real.

Circle your best 𝒰.

On Your Own Write a sentence about unicorns.

Yaks are good swimmers.

Yaks are good swimmers.

Trace and write.

Y Y Y Y Y

Y is joined to the letter that follows. Write words that begin with *Y*.

Yangtze   Yukon   Yves

Write a sentence that begins with *Y*.

Yaks have long hair.

On Your Own Write a sentence that begins with *Y*.

72

Circle Z and *Z* in these words.

Zebras live in Zimbabwe.

Zebras live in Zimbabwe.

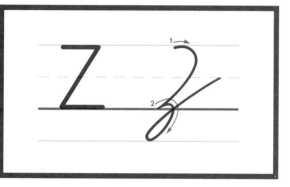

Trace and write.

Z Z Z Z Z

Z is joined to the letter that follows. Write words that begin with *Z*.

Zambia   *Zurich*   *Zoe*

Write a sentence that begins with *Z*.

Zebras have stripes.

On Your Own Write a sentence about zebras.

Circle your best *Z*.

Review

Write names of national parks.

Yosemite   *Zion*

Yellowstone

Circle your best uppercase letter.

Write these sentences.

Ursula went to Yosemite.

Zion is in Utah.

Circle your best word.

74

Circle V and $\mathcal{V}$ in these words.

Vultures fly high in the sky.

Vultures fly high in the sky.

V $\mathcal{V}$

Trace and write.

$\mathcal{V}$ $\mathcal{V}$ $\mathcal{V}$ $\mathcal{V}$ $\mathcal{V}$ $\mathcal{V}$

$\mathcal{V}$ is not joined to the letter that follows. Write words that begin with $\mathcal{V}$.

Venus   Volga   Vittorio

Write a sentence that begins with $\mathcal{V}$.

Vultures are large birds.

On Your Own Write a sentence that begins with $\mathcal{V}$.

Circle your best $\mathcal{V}$.

X-ray fish are as clear as glass.

X-ray fish are as clear as glass.

Trace and write.

$\mathcal{X}$ $\mathcal{X}$ $\mathcal{X}$ $\mathcal{X}$ $\mathcal{X}$ $\mathcal{X}$

$\mathcal{X}$ is not joined to the letter that follows. Write words that begin with $\mathcal{X}$.

Xian   Xaviera   Xerxes

Write a sentence that begins with $\mathcal{X}$.

X-ray fish are tiny.

On Your Own Write a sentence that begins with $\mathcal{X}$.

Circle your best $\mathcal{X}$.

Circle **W** and *W* in these words.

Walruses live on floating ice.

Walruses live on floating ice.

W *W*

Trace and write.

W   W   W   W   W

W is not joined to the letter that follows. Write words that begin with *W* .

Wednesday   Wild West

Write a sentence that begins with *W* .

Walruses eat clams.

On Your Own Write a sentence about the Wild West.

Circle your best *W* .

Review

Write names of cities.

Vancouver   Xenia   Wuhan

Venice   Warsaw

Circle your best uppercase letter.

Write these sentences.

Xiao is from Xiang.

Circle your best word.

We read about Vienna.

Circle T and _T_ in these words.

Tigers usually hunt at night.

Tigers usually hunt at night.

Trace and write.

$\mathcal{T}$ $\mathcal{T}$ $\mathcal{T}$ $\mathcal{T}$ $\mathcal{T}$

$\mathcal{T}$ is not joined to the letter that follows. Write words that begin with $\mathcal{T}$.

Tuesday   Thursday   Tai

Write a sentence that begins with $\mathcal{T}$.

The tiger has stripes.

On Your Own Write a sentence about tigers.

Circle your best $\mathcal{T}$.

Circle F and *F* in these words.

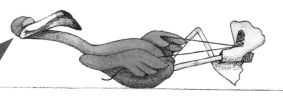

Flamingos have webbed feet.

Flamingos have webbed feet.

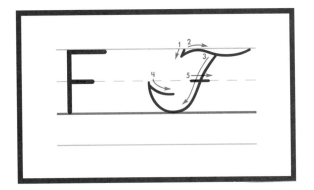

Trace and write.

F F F F F

F is not joined to the letter that follows. Write words that begin with *F*.

February   Friday   Faye

Write a sentence that begins with *F*.

Flamingos eat shellfish.

On Your Own Write a sentence about flamingos.

Circle your best *F*.

80

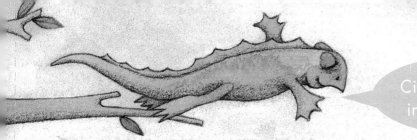

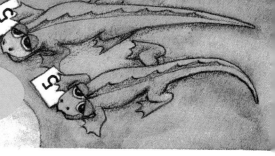

Circle I and *I*
in these words.

Iguanas drop from trees into water.

Iguanas drop from trees into water.

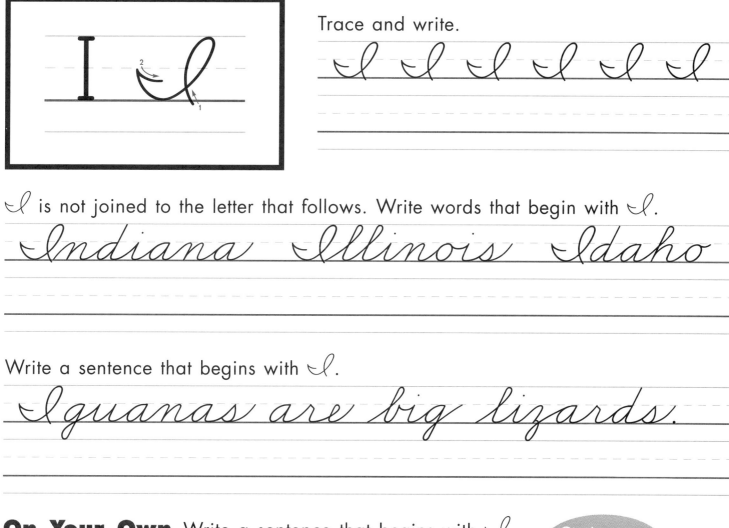

Trace and write.

I is not joined to the letter that follows. Write words that begin with *I*.

Indiana   Illinois   Idaho

Write a sentence that begins with *I*.

Iguanas are big lizards.

On Your Own Write a sentence that begins with *I*.

Circle your best *I*.

Circle J and *J* in these words.

Jaguars have many spots.

Jaguars have many spots.

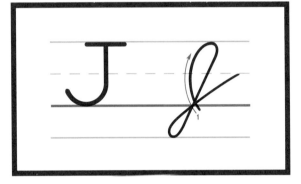

J J

Trace and write.

J J J J J J

J is joined to the letter that follows. Write words that begin with *J*.

January   June   July

Write a sentence that begins with *J*.

Jaguars live in jungles.

On Your Own Write a sentence about January, June, or July.

Circle your best *J*.

Quails are found in Quebec.

Quails are found in Quebec.

Trace and write.

Q Q Q Q Q Q Q

Q is not joined to the letter that follows. Write words that begin with *Q*.

Quebec   Qatar   Quincy

Write a sentence that begins with *Q*.

Quetzals are birds, too.

On Your Own Write a sentence that begins with *Q*.

Review

Write names of countries.

Japan   France   India

Thailand   Qatar

Circle your best uppercase letter.

Write these sentences.

Jordan is next to Israel.

Fran is from Italy.

Circle your best word.

Manuscript Maintenance: Secret Code

The answer to each riddle is written in code. Write the correct letters using your best uppercase manuscript.

1	2	3	4	5	6	7	8	9	10	11	12	13
Z	A	Y	B	X	C	W	D	V	E	U	F	T

14	15	16	17	18	19	20	21	22	23	24	25	26
G	S	H	R	I	Q	J	P	K	O	L	N	M

What animal talks a lot? 3 2 22

YAK

You use this animal to play baseball. 4 2 13

What kind of animal has a key, but doesn't open a door? 8 23 25 22 10 3

What type of fish is the richest? 14 23 24 8 12 18 15 16

What bird is present at every meal? 15 7 2 24 24 23 7

The alphabet goes from A to Z. What animal goes from Z to A? 1 10 4 17 2

What do camels have that no other animals have? 4 2 4 3   6 2 26 10 24 15

Circle G and 𝒢 in these words.

Geese fly south for the winter.

Geese fly south for the winter.

SOUTH

Trace and write.

𝒢 𝒢 𝒢 𝒢 𝒢

𝒢 is not joined to the letter that follows. Write words that begin with 𝒢.

Georgia   Grace   Garth

Write a sentence that begins with 𝒢.

Gulls steal goose eggs.

On Your Own Write a sentence that begins with 𝒢.

Circle your best 𝒢.

86

Circle S and 𝒮 in these words.

Seals are excellent swimmers.

Seals are excellent swimmers.

Trace and write.

𝒮 𝒮 𝒮 𝒮 𝒮

𝒮 is not joined to the letter that follows. Write words that begin with 𝒮.

Saturday   Sunday

Write a sentence that begins with 𝒮.

Seals have smooth coats.

On Your Own Write a sentence about seals.

Circle your best 𝒮.

Llamas are related to camels.

Llamas are related to camels.

Trace and write.

L   L   L   L

L is not joined to the letter that follows. Write words that begin with *L*.

London   Little League

Write a sentence that begins with *L*.

Llamas have long necks.

On Your Own Write a sentence that begins with *L*.

Circle your best *L*.

88

Circle D and $\mathcal{D}$ in these words.

Dogs need to exercise every day.

Dogs need to exercise every day.

Trace and write.

$\mathcal{D}$ $\mathcal{D}$ $\mathcal{D}$ $\mathcal{D}$ $\mathcal{D}$ $\mathcal{D}$

$\mathcal{D}$ is not joined to the letter that follows. Write words that begin with $\mathcal{D}$.

December   Dalmatian

Write a sentence that begins with $\mathcal{D}$.

Dogs are loyal pets.

On Your Own Write a sentence about dogs.

Circle your best $\mathcal{D}$.

89

Review

Write names of deserts.

Death Valley   Gibson

Sahara   Libyan

Circle your best uppercase letter.

Write these sentences.

Sol saw the Great Sandy.

Li saw the Gobi.

Circle your best word.

Circle P and *P* in these words.

Porcupines have many sharp quills.

Porcupines have many sharp quills.

Trace and write.

P   P   P   P   P

P is not joined to the letter that follows. Write words that begin with *P*.

Pluto   Paris   Pierre   Pru

Write a sentence that begins with *P*.

Porcupines are rodents.

Circle your best *P*.

On Your Own Write a sentence about porcupines.

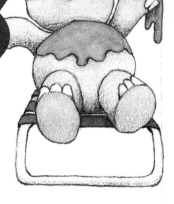

Circle R and *R* in these words.

Rhinos use mud to block the sun.

Rhinos use mud to block the sun.

Trace and write.

R   R   R   R   R

R is joined to the letter that follows. Write words that begin with *R*.

Rome   Rhine River   Ray

Write a sentence that begins with *R*.

Rain keeps rhinos cool.

On Your Own Write a sentence that begins with *R*.

Circle your best *R*.

Circle B and *B* in these words.

Baboons carry food in their cheeks.

Baboons carry food in their cheeks.

Trace and write.

B B B B B

B is not joined to the letter that follows. Write words that begin with *B*.

Badlands Beijing Brett

Write a sentence that begins with *B*.

Baby baboons need care.

Circle your best *B*.

On Your Own Write a sentence about baboons.

93

Review

Write names of state capitals.

Phoenix   Raleigh

Circle your best uppercase letter.

Richmond   Boise

Write these sentences.

Ryan moved to Boston.

Circle your best word.

Please come to Pierre.

Review Uppercase Letters

Write these uppercase letters in cursive.

A E C O

K X M Y Z

V W N H U

T F Q I J

D G L S

B R P

JOINING ALERT

Remember! These letters are joined to the letter that follows.

R K H J U A
Y C M Z E N

These letters are not.

G F O S T X B
Q L D P I V W

Write these words in cursive.

Memorial Day

Grand Canyon

United Nations

Puerto Rico

Circle your best word.

I can write in cursive.

Keys to Legibility

You've learned to write lowercase and uppercase cursive letters. Now you're on your own. Write a sentence in cursive.

_____

_____

_____

_____

In the following pages, you will write more words and sentences in cursive. You will look again at the size and shape of your letters. You will also improve your slant and spacing to help make your writing easy to read.

Keys to Legibility: Slant

Help make your writing easy to read. Pay attention to slant.

Cursive letters have a forward slant.

a $\mathcal{A}$ $\mathcal{y}$ $\mathcal{Z}$

POSITION Check your paper position.
PULL Pull your downstrokes in the right direction.
SHIFT Shift your paper as you write.

If you are left-handed . . .

pull toward your left elbow.

If you are right-handed . . .

pull toward your midsection.

Draw lines through the slant strokes in the letters.

Check the slant.

This is uneven slant.

This is good slant.

97

Keys to Legibility: Spacing

Help make your writing easy to read.
Pay attention to letter and word spacing.

This between spacing is just right.

This word spacing is just right.

Is there space for *o* between letters?

spacing   spacing

Write the word correctly.

Is there space for \ between words?

Isthiseasytoread?

Is this easy to read?

Is this easy to read?

Write the sentence correctly.

Looking at Letter Size and Shape

Where can you find each animal? Write the name of the continent.

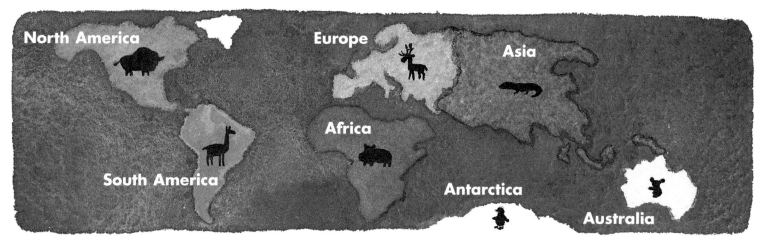

North America   *Antarctica*   *Australia*
Europe   *Africa*   *South America*   *Asia*

L E G I B L E LETTERS

Remember! Tall letters touch the headline.
Short letters touch the midline.
Letters with descenders go below the baseline.

bison

penguin

koala

llama

Komodo dragon

hippopotamus

Circle the name
you wrote best.

reindeer

Looking at Slant

What do you hear when a dog barks? Write the sound words in different languages.

English

POSITION
PULL
SHIFT

Remember! Check the way you hold your pencil and place your paper.

Rruf-ruf

Gruf-gruf
Russian

English

French

German

Japanese

Russian

Spanish

Won-won

Japanese

Whow-whow

French

Draw lines through the slant strokes.

Guau-guau

Spanish

Vrow-vrow

German

100

Looking at Letter Spacing

Write the name of each group of animals.

a cloud of gnats   *a knot of toads*
a school of fish   *a bed of clams*

LEGIBLE LETTERS   *This better spacing is just right.*

Is there space for *o* between letters?

On Your Own Make up a name for a group of skunks.

Looking at Word Spacing

Laugh it up! Write the answer to each joke.

LEGIBLE LETTERS   *This word spacing is just right.*

What is gray and has four legs and a trunk?

_____

_____

_____

What is as big as an elephant but weighs nothing?

_____

_____

_____

How do you make an elephant float?

_____

_____

_____

What time is it when an elephant sits in your seat?

_____

_____

_____

with ice cream and milk

a mouse on vacation

an elephant's shadow

time to get a new seat

Is there space for \ between words?

I've Got a Dog

I've got a dog
   as thin as a rail,
He's got fleas
   all over his tail;
Every time his tail
   goes flop,
The fleas on the bottom
   all hop to the top.

Write this poem in your best cursive handwriting.
Pay attention to size and shape, slant, and spacing.

Circle your best line of writing.

Manuscript Maintenance: Word Math

Add and subtract words to make a new word.
Here is a sample to help you get started.

free   +   log   -   eel   =   frog

Write your answers in manuscript.

man + tops - ant = _____

fowl + ox - owl = _____

grape + sew - apes = _____

grain + oat - rain = _____

herb + earring - bear = _____

On Your Own Write a word math problem of your own.

_____

_____

_____

Looking at Letter Size and Shape

Write the name of a story in which you can find each animal.

 *Henny Penny*   *The Three Bears*

 Little Red Riding Hood

L E G I B L E
LETTERS

Remember! Tall letters touch the headline.
Short letters touch the midline.
Letters with descenders go below the baseline.

Who's been eating
my porridge?

The better to eat
you with, my dear!

The sky is falling!

Circle the title
you wrote best.

On Your Own Write the name of a favorite story.

Looking at Slant

Write the name of each animal champion.

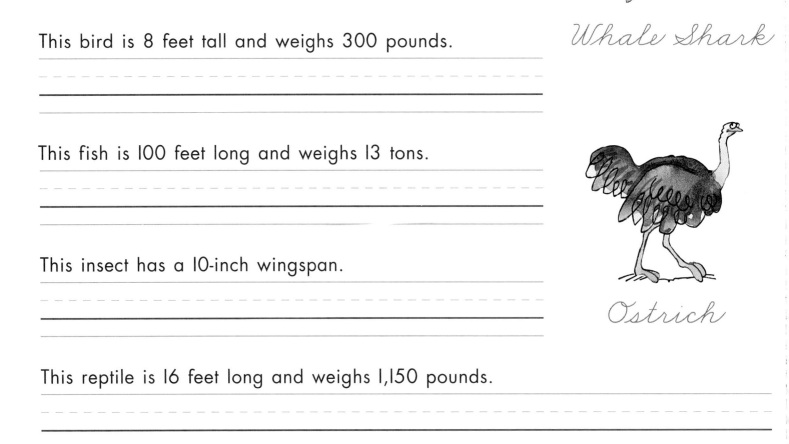

POSITION
PULL
SHIFT

Remember! Check the way you hold your pencil and place your paper.

Whale Shark

This bird is 8 feet tall and weighs 300 pounds.

This fish is 100 feet long and weighs 13 tons.

This insect has a 10-inch wingspan.

Ostrich

This reptile is 16 feet long and weighs 1,150 pounds.

Check your slant.

Atlas Moth

Draw lines through the slant strokes in the letters.

Saltwater Crocodile

Looking at Letter Spacing

IDIOMS

An idiom is an expression that does not mean exactly what it says. Use animal idioms. Write each one next to its meaning.

barking up the wrong tree
letting the cat out of the bag

raining cats and dogs
in the doghouse

LEGIBLE LETTERS   *This better spacing is just right.*

telling a secret

making a mistake

raining hard

in trouble

Is there space for *o* between letters?

107

Looking at Word Spacing

Say each tongue twister three times as fast as you can. Then write it.

LEGIBLE LETTERS

This word spacing is just right.

Little lemmings like lots of lemons.

Monkeys mix millions of muffins.

Dalmatian digs dozens of daylilies.

Is there space for ＼ between words?

On Your Own Write a tongue twister you know.

If You Ever Meet a Whale

If you ever, ever,
  ever meet a whale,
You must never, never
  grab him by his tail.
If you ever, ever
  grab him by his tail—
You will never, never
  meet another whale.

Write this poem in your best cursive handwriting.
Pay attention to size and shape, slant, and spacing.

Circle your best line of writing.

So Much

I have so much to say
And so much to write.
I want every word
To be written just right!

So Much
I have so much to say
And so much to write.
I want every word
To be written just right!

Write the poem in your best cursive handwriting.

Circle your best
line of writing.

Record of Student's Handwriting Skills

Cursive

	Needs Improvement	Shows Mastery
Sits correctly	☐	☐
Holds pencil correctly	☐	☐
Positions paper correctly	☐	☐
Writes undercurve strokes	☐	☐
Writes downcurve strokes	☐	☐
Writes overcurve strokes	☐	☐
Writes slant strokes	☐	☐
Writes **i, t, u, w**	☐	☐
Writes **r, s, p, j**	☐	☐
Writes **a, c, d, q, g, o**	☐	☐
Writes numerals **1–10**	☐	☐
Writes **n, m, x, y, z, v**	☐	☐
Writes **e, l, h, k, f, b**	☐	☐
Writes **A, C, E, O**	☐	☐
Writes **N, M, K, H**	☐	☐
Writes **U, Y, Z**	☐	☐
Writes **V, X, W**	☐	☐
Writes **T, F**	☐	☐
Writes **I, J, Q**	☐	☐
Writes **G, S, L, D**	☐	☐
Writes **P, R, B**	☐	☐

	Needs Improvement	Shows Mastery
Writes the undercurve to undercurve joining	☐	☐
Writes the undercurve to downcurve joining	☐	☐
Writes the undercurve to overcurve joining	☐	☐
Writes the overcurve to undercurve joining	☐	☐
Writes the overcurve to downcurve joining	☐	☐
Writes the overcurve to overcurve joining	☐	☐
Writes the checkstroke to undercurve joining	☐	☐
Writes the checkstroke to downcurve joining	☐	☐
Writes the checkstroke to overcurve joining	☐	☐
Writes with correct size and shape	☐	☐
Writes with correct slant	☐	☐
Writes with correct spacing	☐	☐
Regularly checks written work for legibility	☐	☐

Index